we would see Jesus

BY Kenton K. Smith

52 COMMUNION MEDITATIONS

Cincinnati, Ohio

Library of Congress Cataloging-in-Publication Data

Smith, Kenton K.
    We would see Jesus : meditations for the Communion service / by
Kenton K. Smith.
        p.   cm.
    Includes indexes.
    ISBN 0-7847-0785-5 (pbk.)
    1. Lord's Supper—Meditations. 2. Devotional calendars.
I. Title.
BV826.5.S65   1998
264' .36—dc21

The Standard Publishing Company, Cincinnati, Ohio
A division of Standex International Corporation
© 1998 by The Standard Publishing Company
All rights reserved
Printed in the United States of America
05 04   03 02 01 00 99 98   5 4 3 2 1

Introduction

What is the purpose of Communion? Is it merely to remind us that what we are doing is a continuation of a service Jesus instituted two thousand years ago? Are we only to be concerned with making certain that worshipers are "discerning the Lord's body" (1 Corinthians 11:29, KJV) and blood?

These are worthy aims and not to be neglected. But we sometimes fail to see the richness of the Lord's Supper in what it can teach us and how it can mold us. The meditation can lead us to think about our sins and our Savior, our struggles with holiness on earth and our hopes of Heaven to come, our need for restoration of fellowship with brothers and sisters at odds with us, and our evangelistic challenges.

The meditations in this book have been designed to stimulate such thinking. Some of them may make hearers feel a bit uncomfortable. However, it is dangerous to be comfortable at Communion time, if that comfort comes at the expense of neglecting penitence, holiness, and God's call to diligent service.

Several meditations tie in with special days on the calendar. Others are connected with certain occupations that may be represented in the church membership. Some of the best meditations I have heard featured the speaker's using work experiences as illustrations of Communion-related truths.

Each meditation includes a related Scripture, a suggested hymn, and some brief prayer thoughts. It is my hope that speakers will use and adapt these to prepare thought-provoking meditations. The Lord's Supper is worthy of our very best effort.

—Kenton K. Smith

CONTENTS

SPECIAL DAYS

(Note: The numbers indicate the meditation number.)

OCCUPATIONS

A SHOCKING SACRIFICE

GENESIS 22:1, 2, 9-12

God commanded a man to offer his son as a burnt offering! That is surely a disturbing and shocking biblical story. The man was of course Abraham, and the son was Isaac. The account concludes with God's sparing Isaac after Abraham demonstrated his willingness to obey even so difficult a command.

That account is meant to disturb us. It is an early hint in the Bible of the shocking sacrifice God would make on our behalf. He gave His own Son to be a sin offering for us, and that fact should continually amaze and shake us.

Hebrews 11:19 indicates that Abraham was ready to sacrifice Isaac in the confidence that God would raise the lad back to life. Such confidence could not have made it any easier for Abraham to perform the task. God gave up Jesus Christ to the cross, knowing that His Son would rise from the dead. Again, however, that could not have made the heavenly Father's sacrifice easier.

It must have been painful for Abraham to view the bewilderment and terror in Isaac's eyes as he, Isaac's own father, raised the knife, ready to plunge it into his son's heart. It must have grieved the heavenly Father to hear His only begotten Son cry out, "My God, my God, why have You forsaken me?"

HYMN

"At Calvary"

Mercy there was great, and grace was free; Pardon there was multiplied to me;

There my burdened soul found liberty, At Calvary.

~William R. Newell

The Lord's Supper depicts the heavenly Father's shocking sacrifice of His Son. How can we ever approach this part of our worship in a careless, matter-of-fact attitude? Let us instead partake in amazement and in renewed appreciation of that tremendous act of sacrifice.

PRAYER

Our loving heavenly Father, we are awed by what You have given for us! Help us to feel the shock Jesus' followers must have felt when He died. Beyond that, help us to understand the magnitude of Your sacrifice. In Jesus' name, amen.

A SIGNIFICANT SUPPER

MATTHEW 6:33

What is happening in the world at this moment? Is it possible that as we assemble here, a group of diplomats is meeting in a secret location, desperately trying to avoid a bloody war? Perhaps a team of scientists is on the brink of discovering a drug that will cure all kinds of cancer. In the Holy Land an archaeologist may be in the process of making the find of the century.

We can say without hesitation that nothing more important is happening than what we are doing. Consider that the Lord's Supper takes us back to the two most important events in history: the crucifixion of Christ and His resurrection. Consider that this supper points ahead to the most important event yet to come: Christ's return. How can anything be more important than this observance?

And yet, people are absent from this table for trivial reasons. We feel we must extend hospitality when we have guests at our house, but the entertaining of company should not keep us from Communion. Neither should having laundry to do, a lawn to mow, homework to complete rival the importance of meeting our Lord around His table.

A Communion meditation should not merely induce guilt in the minds of worshipers who have been careless about their attendance at the Lord's table. The past cannot be changed, but the future can. If you have been permitting anything else to take priority over communing with the Lord, now is the time to change that. Recognize that Communion is the most significant thing you can do on Sunday, and treat it as such.

PRAYER

We thank You, heavenly Father, for this supremely important observance of the Lord's Supper. Make us constantly aware of its significance. Help us to give it the priority that it merits. In Jesus' name, amen.

An Evangelistic Communion

1 Peter 3:15

To a great extent Communion is a very personal, one-to-one relationship with our Savior. But looked at another way, it is an act that bears testimony to others regarding our crucified Lord, and is a demonstration of the gospel with evangelistic implications.

As we prepare to eat the bread and drink the juice, we may well ask ourselves, "Who among my family, friends, and acquaintances need to know of the crucified Christ depicted in these emblems?" And it is quite in keeping with our personal. Communion if we picture those unsaved ones arising from the waters of the baptistery and then seated near us sharing the same bread and juice that we partake of. The words of a hymn seem especially significant here: "Oh, that my Savior were your Savior, too!"

Surely one effect of communing with our Lord should be a sense of evangelistic urgency. The verse of Scripture we read earlier indicates that we should always be prepared to speak to others about our hope in Christ. Our moments at the Lord's table contribute to such preparation. We should come away from this table with our tongues and lips primed to proclaim our Lord's gift of salvation.

Hymn

"I Am Praying for You"

I have a Savior, He's pleading in glory, A dear, loving Savior, tho' earth friends be few;

And now He is watching in tenderness o'er me, But oh, that my Savior were your Savior, too!

~S. O'Malley Cluff

Let us make this an evangelistic Communion with an evangelistic commitment. In our meditation and in our partaking may we promise our Lord that we will do a more faithful job of sharing the news of His tortured body, shed blood, death, and resurrection. And may we make this week a powerful period of promise keeping.

PRAYER

Our gracious Father, we enjoy these moments of communing with Your Son, and it is very appropriate that we do so. But in enjoying this privilege may we remember our responsibility. Inspire us here with the urgency of sharing Christ's message of salvation with others this week. In His name, amen.

BEHOLDING THE BEAUTY OF JESUS

ISAIAH 33: 17

Once again we behold the beauty of springtime in the variety of colors we see in nature. Tulips come in various colors, but we may think first of red ones. The familiar purple hyacinth is but one of many hues in which that flower appears. When we think of daffodils, we picture them as creamy yellow.

In the midwestern United States, spring is the occasion for the robin's return. Whoever described this creature as "robin redbreast" must have been color blind. Nevertheless, we appreciate the robin's reddish-orange underside.

Let us rejoice in nature's colors. Then let us think of the beauty of Jesus in terms of colors. Red reminds us of His blood shed for our sins. White symbolizes His purity. Green speaks of new life and thereby represents the newness of life we gain through His atonement. Blue, the color of heaven, is a reminder of the heavenly Jerusalem being prepared by Jesus as an eternal home for us.

In the Lord's Supper we behold the beauty of Jesus. The whiteness of the loaf and the red of the juice symbolize His purity and His sacrifice. In the words, "Do this in remembrance of me," we perceive the beauty of His gracious invitation to commune with Him. As we partake we

HYMN

"Fairest Lord Jesus"

Fairest Lord Jesus! Ruler of all nature! O Thou of God and man the Son! Thee will I cherish, Thee will I honor, Thou, my soul's glory, joy, and crown!

~Joseph A. Seiss

enjoy a moment of beautiful unity, sharing in the one loaf and the one cup.

The reminders of His beauty are all around us. Let us behold in awe and gratitude.

PRAYER

Our Father in Heaven, we praise You for Your beauty and that of Your Son Jesus. During this past week we have beheld much that is ugly and sickening, and we will soon look on more of the same. But now envelop our minds and hearts in the inexpressible beauty of our Savior. In His name we pray. Amen.

BYPASSING THE BUNNIES AND BASKETS

ACTS 2:22-24

We have to put a lot of distractions from our minds when we commune with our Lord on Easter Sunday. This is a holiday season. It features songs about Easter bunnies; baskets of candy; Easter egg hunts; dressing up in bright, new outfits; and gathering for family dinners. Somehow we must mentally bypass all of that right now to focus on a crucified and risen Savior.

Of course, distractions at the Lord's table are not unusual. On any given Sunday, other matters may vie for our attention. Perhaps we are worried about a crisis developing at our place of work. We may be excited about an upcoming party or ball game or meeting with old friends. It is possible that an experience we have had, favorable or unfavorable, in this church building today is dominating our thoughts.

We may need to pray, "Lord, deliver me from distractions! Help me to concentrate on communing with my Savior." If the bunnies and baskets or any other comparatively trivial matters interfere with our meditation, we can use an act of will to overcome them. By deliberately centering our thoughts on Jesus, on His cross and His empty tomb, we can simply leave no room for distractions.

HYMN

"Lead Me to Calvary"

Lest I forget Gethsemane; Lest I forget Thine agony; Lest I forget Thy love for me, Lead me to Calvary.

~Jennie E. Hussey

At no time during the week is it more important to take charge of our minds and focus our thoughts. Let us be one hundred percent present at the Lord's table.

PRAYER

Our wise and wonderful Father in Heaven, we praise You for the dramatic story of Christ's death, burial, and resurrection. We remember that story today, as we do each Sunday of the year. The world has its ways of celebrating Easter, and we share in these to a certain extent. But help us never to lose sight of the basic truths of the gospel that these emblems depict. In Jesus' name, amen.

CAN WE SEE CALVARY?

LUKE 23:32, 33

Professor Willard Winter at Cincinnati Bible College used to challenge his students to use their "sanctified imaginators." That meant the students were to utilize the power of imagination to picture biblical events. No biblical event merits the application of imaginative power more than the crucifixion of Christ. As we prepare our hearts for communing, let us try to see Calvary.

Picture Jesus as He arrives at Calvary. Already the crown of thorns is on His head, and rivulets of blood are coursing down His face. His back, subjected to scourging, is a sickening mass of torn, bloody tissue. Exhaustion is evident in His drawn face and sagging shoulders.

Picture Jesus as He is nailed to the cross. We wince as we imagine the spikes driven through His hands and the one spike that apparently pierces both feet and pins them together against the cross. Once the nails are in place, the executioners lift the cross and drop it into a hole prepared for it. We shudder as we imagine the jarring and the vibrating flesh pulling against the unyielding nails.

Picture Jesus as He hangs on the cross. The muscles are knotting in His neck and upper back as the result of His arms being outstretched. He struggles to breathe, because the

HYMN

"When I Survey the Wondrous Cross"

When I survey the wondrous cross, On which the Prince of glory died, My richest gain I count but loss, And pour contempt on all my pride.

~Isaac Watts

awkward position of His body exerts extreme pressure on His lungs.

Picture Jesus as His body is removed from the cross. That body is limp, lifeless, blood-stained, and ravaged by human cruelty. We can almost hear the wails and the sobs of those who loved Him and see the sad procession to the nearby garden tomb. But today we can rejoice, because we know that tomb was a very temporary resting place for Jesus' body.

Prayer

Our Father, stir up our minds to a vivid remembrance of what Your Son endured for us on Calvary. In His name, amen.

CARRIERS OF THE CROSS

MARK 15:21

Only John's Gospel speaks of Jesus "carrying his own cross." In the other three accounts, we learn of Simon of Cyrene. He apparently reached Jerusalem just as the cruel procession to Calvary got underway. Jesus, weakened by scourging, bore the cross a short way before stumbling under its weight. The Roman soldiers probably picked Simon at random to shoulder the cross for the remainder of the journey.

Simon has been the focus of certain questions. Did he carry the cross willingly or grudgingly? Did his part in the drama of Calvary lead him to belief in Christ? The fact that Mark mentions his sons Alexander and Rufus suggests that they were Christians, and possibly Simon was as well.

We do not know what happened to Simon afterward, but we do know this: he was a carrier of the cross. Perhaps we envy him that. We may say to ourselves, "If I had been there, I would gladly have assisted my Savior in bearing the weight of the cross."

The cross represented Jesus' mission. It was not necessary for our redemption that He struggle under its burden on the way to Calvary. But it was essential, once He and the cross arrived at that hill of horror, that He be nailed to it and suffer and die upon it.

HYMN

"Must Jesus Bear the Cross Alone?"

Must Jesus bear the cross alone, And all the world go free? No; there's a cross for ev'ry one, And there's a cross for me.

~Thomas Shepherd

We are unable to help Jesus carry His cross to Calvary. However, we can share in His mission. He declared in Luke 19:10 that He came to seek and save the lost. In that sense we can be carriers of the cross. It is our privilege to carry the message of salvation through the cross to the lost in our time.

PRAYER

Our gracious Father, thank You for the message of the cross depicted in this Communion. As we remember the cross, help us more clearly see our part in Jesus' mission. In His name, amen.

CLEANSING YOUR CONSCIENCE

HEBREWS 9:13, 14

Christians seem to suffer as much from the guilt of old, partially-buried sins as non-Christians do. They may require the services of psychiatrists as often as non-Christians. They may try to dull the voice of conscience with tranquilizers as frequently as those who are outside of Christ. This simply should not be.

Confession of faith in Christ and penitent submission to baptism certainly do not erase all traces of guilt. But when we follow up on our baptism with weekly participation in the Lord's Supper, the burden of guilt should eventually fall away and leave us free. Why has that not happened? Perhaps we have not emphasized enough that the blood of Jesus Christ cleanses our conscience.

It may help us to picture our conscience as a house with many rooms. In one room inch-thick dust and cobwebs represent lies we told as a child. Another room features stained walls and a filthy carpet. It symbolizes a hidden sexual sin. Finally, we open another door and find the air greasy and foul smelling. We know that this points back to an occasion on which we hurt another person's feelings.

Communion is an appropriate occasion for spiritual housecleaning. Let us get rid of that dust, those cobwebs, the stains and filth, and

HYMN

"Cleanse Me"

Search me, O God, and know my heart today; Try me; O Savior, know my thoughts, I pray; See if there be some wicked way in me; Cleanse me from ev'ry sin, and set me free.

~J. Edwin Orr

the foul odors. One cleansing agent can handle all that: the shed blood of Jesus Christ. As we partake of the loaf and the cup, let us picture the "rooms of our conscience" becoming clean, spotless, and bright.

PRAYER

Our gracious heavenly Father, we praise You for forgiving us. But somehow the burden of guilt continues to weigh us down. The memory of old sin persists in soiling our conscience. At this table with its vivid symbols of our forgiveness and cleansing, let us gain a complete victory over the ravages of personal guilt. In Jesus' name, amen.

COMMUNING AND FORGIVING

MATTHEW 5:23, 24

Jesus was describing Old Testament worship when He said, "Leave your gift there in front of the altar. " But today He may be saying to New Testament worshipers, "Before you partake of the bread and the cup make up your mind that you will take the first opportunity to resolve the conflict you have with another person."

Is there another worshiper today toward whom you hold a grudge? You need to see him or her as soon as today's worship has concluded and say, "I am sorry for the misunderstanding between us. Please forgive me for what I said or did. I am prepared to forgive you, if that is your wish. " In this way you can partake of the bread and the juice more joyously.

Is there a neighbor, fellow worker, or schoolmate with whom you are at odds? Use your telephone or meet this person face-to-face and deal boldly and charitably with the problem between you. Say, "I do not want this matter to stand between us. I regret what I said or did to offend you, and I ask your forgiveness. If you wish for me to forgive you, then for Jesus' sake I will do it."

Communing and forgiving are spiritual acts that must be bound together. Let us clear the lines of communion with our Savior by practicing total forgiveness.

HYMN

"More Like the Master"

More like the Master I would ever be, More of His meekness, more humility; More zeal to labor, more courage to be true, More consecration for work He bids me do.

~Charles H. Gabriel

PRAYER

Dear heavenly Father, thank You for the forgiveness we have gained through Christ. As we again share in the Lord's Supper, impress us with the realization that we are not worthy of our forgiveness. Help us likewise to forgive others, even when part of us insists that they are not worthy or deserving of forgiveness. Give us the grace to ask forgiveness of those we have offended. In Jesus' name, amen.

COMMUNION QUESTIONS

EXODUS 12:26, 27

Do you remember the first time you witnessed a Communion service? Perhaps you were a child, sitting in an adult worship service. Perhaps you were an adult, visiting a church on Sunday morning and observing what seemed to you a strange ceremony. You had questions, but you were hesitant to ask them.

Moses instructed Israel in regard to the Passover, "And when your children ask you, 'What does this ceremony mean to you?' then tell them, 'It is the Passover sacrifice to the Lord ...'" (Exodus 12:26, 27). The Passover meal was sure to raise questions in the minds of little ones, and the adults were to give careful answers. The Lord's Supper should likewise be an occasion for fruitful questions and answers.

Visitors may hesitate to ask such questions. When the emblems are passed, they wonder if they should partake. Many churches take the position that it is Jesus' supper, and they do not have the right to invite or debar. But they usually emphasize that the Lord's Supper is for Christians.

Visitors may also ponder why we partake of Communion as often as we do. The New Testament nowhere contains a command to observe it yearly or quarterly or monthly or weekly. But the example of the church at Troas

HYMN

"Tell Me the Old, Old Story"

Tell me the Old, Old Story, Of unseen things above, Of Jesus and His glory, Of Jesus and His love; Tell me the story simply, As to a little child, For I am weak and weary, And helpless and defiled.

~A. Catherine Hankey

in Acts 20:7 points to the breaking of bread as a central part of Sunday worship. It is reasonable to assume that it should be a central part of every Sunday's worship.

If you have questions about Communion, ask them. Ministers and elders are eager to explain the biblical teaching behind our Communion service. And the Lord's Supper is too important to approach in ignorance.

PRAYER

Dear heavenly Father, we praise You for this simple meal that holds profound significance. Help us all to grow in our understanding of it. In Jesus' name, amen.

DYING FOR THE UNDESERVING

ROMANS 5:6-8

Most of us have probably seen a certain news video many times: a smiling president Ronald Reagan, preparing to get into his limousine …the sound of shots …turmoil and confusion …a man being pinned to the sidewalk by Secret Service agents.

President Reagan survived that assassination attempt in March of 1981. But he probably would not have survived without the Secret Service. Their job is to protect the president of the United States, and agents are prepared to die, if necessary, in the line of duty.

Jesus Christ is a kind of one-man Secret Service on our behalf. He died, not to save our physical bodies from death, but to deliver our eternal souls from Hell. His death did not occur as the result of an unanticipated assassination attempt. Instead, Jesus came to earth for the express purpose of dying for us.

But we can draw another important contrast between the United States Secret Service and Jesus Christ. In a sense the president deserves to have people die for him. He is, after all, a great national and world leader. He makes decisions that affect the welfare of the entire human race.

Jesus, on the other hand, died for the undeserving. None of us are righteous enough or

HYMN

"He Died for Me"

Oh, can it be, upon a tree The Savior died for me? My soul is thrilled, My heart is filled, To think He died for me!

~John Newton

good enough to merit the Son of God's death on our behalf. And yet for us, unholy, impure, and unspiritual, He dared to die. Let us partake of His Supper in amazement that He would die for lowly sinners.

PRAYER

We praise You, heavenly Father, for Your grace in sending Jesus to earth, and for His willingness to die for undeserving sinners. May this loaf and cup stir us to amazement and wonder as we remember Him who died for us. We ask it in His name. Amen.

GOOD-BYE WEEPING!
HELLO REJOICING!

PSALM 30:5

Were you weeping last night? Tears can result from sorrow, disappointment, frustration, and pain. Did you experience any of these?

Perhaps you come to the Lord's table with tears still stinging your heart if not your eyes. If so, it is time for weeping to be swallowed up in rejoicing. Jesus Christ has died for your sins! Jesus Christ has risen from the grave! Jesus Christ is here to commune with you! You have abundant reason to rejoice.

This is not an idle exhortation to "forget your troubles, and be happy." It is not a superficial emphasis on positive thinking. It is simply a matter of recognizing that we follow a resurrected Lord who can turn every tragedy into a triumph, every sorrow into a celebration.

The Lord's Supper is itself an appropriate occasion for weeping. The hymn writer pleads, "Stay, let me weep while you whisper, Love paid the ransom for me." When we remember what Jesus suffered for us, and when we contemplate the love that designed our salvation, it should move us to tears.

But the Lord's Supper is an even more appropriate occasion for rejoicing. It speaks of sins forgiven, of a resurrected and coming Lord, of a gospel message we may joyously proclaim, and of eternal victory over death. When we have

HYMN

"Tell Me the Story of Jesus"

Tell me the story of Jesus, Write on my heart ev'ry word; Tell me the story most precious, Sweetest that ever was heard. Tell how the angels in chorus, Sang as they welcomed His birth, "Glory to God in the highest! Peace and good tidings to earth."

~Fanny J. Crosby

finished communing, our tears should be replaced by smiles, our gloom should give way to songs, and our groans should be transformed into hallelujahs.

PRAYER

Our gracious Father in Heaven, thank You for the emotional experience of communing with Your Son. May we weep in sorrow over our sins, and may we rejoice over our redemption. Help us to testify to others by the evidence of our overflowing hearts when we come away from this table. In Jesus' precious name, amen.

How Can We Call This a Supper?

JOHN 6:35

Turkey and dressing, hot bread, heaping bowls of mashed potatoes and green vegetables, pumpkin pie, and fruit salad. To even think of the menu for Thanksgiving dinner is enough to make our mouths water and our stomachs rumble.

Thanksgiving is a time when we acknowledge the good things God has bestowed on us. Perhaps we eat more food on that day than any other day of the year. We may feel sheepish about the way we stuff ourselves and question such indulgence when we realize that countless other human beings are seriously malnourished. On the other hand, we may feel that this one day of overdoing it is excusable, since we share what we have with the needy throughout the year.

But the point we want to make today is that the Lord's Supper seems to contrast with our Thanksgiving dinner. This is a meal consisting only of unleavened bread and grape juice. And each of us partakes of only a tiny amount of these food items. It probably seems ludicrous to an outsider to hear us refer to this as a supper.

But these food items, these emblems, speak of our abundant salvation. They speak of the abundant life Jesus promised in John 10:10: "I have come that they may have life, and have it

HYMN

"A Child of the King"

I'm a child of the King,
A child of the King:
With Jesus my Savior
I'm a child of the King.

~Harriet E. Buell

to the full." They speak of God's abundant provision for our spiritual needs here on earth. Paul said in Ephesians 3:20 that God "is able to do immeasurably more than all we ask or imagine." So there is an abundance here that the eye of flesh cannot see.

PRAYER

Our generous and loving Father, we thank You for material abundance and for spiritual abundance. Help us to accept such abundance with continual gratitude, and help us to share it with others who need it. In Jesus' name, amen.

Is It "Holy Communion"?

1 Corinthians 10: 16, 17

It is not common in our churches to read or hear a reference to "holy Communion." Perhaps the reason is that such a term is not found in the New Testament. We may shy away from it merely because it is used by religious bodies with whose doctrines we take issue. Certainly, however, the term is quite in harmony with biblical teaching.

Its use can be beneficial in several ways. First, it reminds us that the observance itself is holy. Paul's warnings in 1 Corinthians 11 about partaking carelessly and bringing judgment on ourselves speak of the holiness of the Lord's Supper. We must enter this part of our worship with especial reverence and humbleness of mind.

"Holy Communion" also speaks of our need for personal holiness. It is unthinkable that anyone would partake of these emblems and then carelessly indulge in the same old sinful habits and attitudes. We need to join the hymn writer in praying, "More holiness give me," and we need to make a genuine effort to develop holy habits, sanctified speech, and disciplined deeds.

"Holy Communion" reminds us of the holiness of our Savior. The writer of Hebrews refers to Him as "holy, blameless, pure, set apart from sinners, exalted above the heavens" (Hebrews

HYMN

"More Holiness Give Me"

More holiness give me, More striving within; More patience in suf- f'ring, More sorrow for sin; More faith in my Savior, More sense of His care; More joy in His service, More purpose in prayer.

~Philip P. Bliss

7:26). And yet He has made himself approachable to us sinners.

Let us now partake of "holy Communion." And as we do so, let us commit ourselves afresh to holiness of life in imitation of our pure and holy Savior.

PRAYER

Our holy and loving Father, we thank You for the privilege of sharing in this holy observance. Impress us with our need for growth in holiness of life. May this Communion with our Savior be the beginning of a fresh effort to eliminate what is impure and unholy from our lives. In the name of Jesus, amen.

JESUS —CRUCIFIED AGAIN?

HEBREWS 6:4-6

Are you a potential backslider? Can you imagine yourself someday living apart from Christ and His church? Before you exclaim, "I would never let that happen!" think about back-sliders you know. They once gathered with you around the Lord's table, but it has been a long time since they appeared in any church. You would never have imagined that they would now be indulging in ungodly habits and drifting tragically away from Christ.

The Scripture we have read may be the best barrier to backsliding that God has given. It is unthinkable that we would ever be guilty of "crucifying the Son of God all over again and subjecting him to public disgrace." And yet, according to Hebrews 6, that is what we do when we fall away from the faith.

The writer is speaking figuratively. Jesus endured crucifixion once and will never need to do so again. But the idea of public disgrace is very literal. When a Christian rejects Jesus and His church and returns to a life of worldliness, it brings shame on the name and cause of Jesus Christ. Unbelievers whisper to one another, "See, there isn't anything to Christianity. Joe and Jane tried it and now they're back living like regular people."

HYMN

"I Would Be True"

I would be true, for there are those who trust me; I would be pure, for there are those who care; I would be strong, for there is much to suffer; I would be brave, for there is much to dare; I would be brave, for there is much to dare.

~Howard A. Walter

That is only the beginning of the anti-Christian effect of backsliding. Unbelievers are strengthened in their unbelief. Atheists have more fuel for their contention that God, the Bible, and the church are irrelevant today. Young Christians become disillusioned and discouraged. And the devil scores a gleeful triumph.

Let us use the Lord's Supper to fortify ourselves against such backsliding.

PRAYER

Dear Father, we do not want to become backsliders. We are horrified by the thought that we could bring disgrace upon our Savior by returning to a life of unbelief. Help us as we partake of these emblems to develop an ever-stronger bond with You. We ask this in Jesus' name. Amen.

LAMENT FOR
A LOST SON

2 SAMUEL 18:31-33

There is no more poignant scene in the Old Testament than the description of David's reaction to the news of his son Absalom's death. Second Samuel 18:33 records his lament: "O my son Absalom! My son, my son Absalom! If only I had died instead of you—O Absalom, my son, my son!"

If we are familiar with the narrative in 2 Samuel, we may feel amazement at David's reaction. Absalom was headstrong, scheming, and rebellious. He died while trying to overthrow his father as king. His obvious aim was his father's death so that he could replace him as king. Why should David have felt such grief over Absalom's death?

Of course we know the answer. With all Absalom's faults, he was still David's son. The tie between father and son is not easily severed, even when rebellion and strife put a strain on it.

If it was painful for David to bear the news of his son's death, how much more grievous was it for the heavenly Father to experience the death of His only begotten Son! Absalom was rebellious, but Jesus was righteous. Absalom incited warfare and bloodshed, but Jesus brought peace through the blood of His cross. Absalom

HYMN

"My Savior's Love"

How marvelous! how wonderful! And my song shall ever be: How marvelous! how wonderful Is my Savior's love for me! Amen.

~Charles H. Gabriel

aimed for the downfall of his father, but Jesus aimed to do only what pleased His Father.

These Communion emblems remind us of an obedient Son who fulfilled His mission. And they speak to us of a gracious Father who must have suffered tremendous grief in Heaven as He watched His Son dying on a cross.

PRAYER

Our patient and loving Father, we thank You for giving us Your Son. You not only sent Him to earth, but You allowed Him to die on the cruel cross. We praise You as we remember such sacrifice in this Communion. In Jesus' name, amen.

LEARNING HOW TO LOVE

1 JOHN 4:7-12

Our society suffers from serious confusion regarding the matter of love. That confusion is well illustrated by what happens on Valentine's Day. Is love only a matter of sending a cute and colorful card to the one on whom our affections are centered? Does the giving of candy or flowers to our beloved demonstrate a sincere and strong love?

No doubt for some couples this holiday is the occasion for a delightful expression of genuine affection. It is certain, however, that Valentine's Day's brand of "feel-good," frivolous emotional attachment is as far as many people get in developing the practice of love.

More than any card or box of candy or bouquet of flowers, the Lord's table illustrates genuine love. It reminds us that love is sacrificial. God loved us enough to send His Son to earth for us. Jesus Christ loved us enough to give His life for our sins. And we are called to demonstrate the same kind of love to one another: "Dear friends, since God so loved us, we also ought to love one another."

We learn to love, therefore, at this table. As we gather in God's presence, we should rejoice in His love. As we commune with Jesus Christ, we should meditate on His sacrificial love. As we partake of the loaf and the cup, we should

HYMN

"I Love Him Because He First Loved Me"

I love Him because He first loved me, He first loved me, He first loved me; I love Him because He first loved me, And died on the cross of Calvary.

~Frank E. Roush

let these words ring in our hearts: "Dear friends, since God so loved us, we also ought to love one another."

PRAYER

Our loving heavenly Father, we praise You for the revelation of Your love through Jesus Christ. Enlighten us by Your example as to what true love is. May we never be content with expressing only the kind of love the world exults in, but may we learn to love more and more in a Christlike way. In His name, amen.

LESS THAN PERFECT PARTAKERS

GALATIANS 6:14

Imagine this scene: The Communion service is almost over. The trays containing the emblems have been passed among the church members. When the trays are returned to the table, the elders look at them in amazement. None of the bread or juice has been taken by the worshipers. No one felt worthy to partake of the Lord's Supper.

What shall we say about this scene? It has probably never happened, but if the Lord's Supper were really meant only for those worthy of partaking, it should happen. None of us deserve Communion with our Lord.

But then, none of those who partook of the first Communion deserved to do so. Peter partook, and a little later he denied three times that he knew Jesus. James and John were not perfect partakers. Jesus once gave them the nickname "sons of thunder," which apparently referred to their violent tempers. All of the apostles were preoccupied with their own importance on the evening of the first Communion. Jesus had to give them an example of humble service by washing their feet.

In one sense, then, Communion is for those who are unworthy of it. In another sense, God makes us worthy by forgiving our sins. In yet another sense, we make ourselves fit for

HYMN

"Beneath the Cross of Jesus"

I take, O cross, thy shadow For my abiding place; I ask no other sunshine than the sunshine of His face; Content to let the world go by, To know no gain nor loss, My sinful self my only shame, My glory all the cross.

~Elizabeth C. Clephane

partaking by approaching the table in a penitent and humble spirit. If we feel that we "deserve it as much as anyone else" and our focus is on how we are "just as good as anyone else in the church," then it may be best to change that attitude before partaking of the emblems.

PRAYER

We come to this table, heavenly Father, acknowledging our unworthiness. Thank You for extending this privilege to us through the shed blood of Your Son, Jesus. Remind us of our need for constant humility and penitence as we approach this table. We pray in the name of Jesus. Amen.

LINGERING IN THE UPPER ROOM

JOHN 19:16-18

Let us think of that upper room of two thousand years ago. It had no Communion table as such, inscribed with the words, "This do in remembrance of me." There was a feast table laden with roast lamb, herbs, unleavened bread, cups of wine, and other features of the Passover supper. The disciples were not seated in pews, but reclining on couches around the table. Jesus himself spoke the words, "This is my body … This is my blood," instead of an elder quoting them.

It is good to think back to that upper room. What we are about to do today had its beginning there. But we dare not linger in the upper room. It was not there that God made Jesus "to be sin for us"; it was not there that Jesus "redeemed us from the curse of the law." When Jesus instituted the Lord's Supper, He focused His thoughts on the place where His body would be tortured and His blood shed. And that is where our thoughts should be at this time.

But it is surely possible, while caught up in the beauty of the Communion service, to overlook the ugliness of Golgotha to which it points. As we handle our fine Communion ware, we must not forget the roughness of the wood, the sharpness of the nails, the cruelty of the

crown—all part of that scene which soon followed the upper-room gathering.

PRAYER

Our heavenly Father, we thank You for the
beauty of this Communion service. We appreciate the music in the background, the fine
Communion ware, and the convenient size and
shape of the emblems. But help us never to lose
sight of the brutality and ugliness of Jesus' crucifixion, to which this service points. In Jesus'
precious name, amen.

LORD, SEND US AN EARTHQUAKE

MATTHEW 27:50,51; 28:1,2

Have you ever noticed what a significant role earthquakes played in the New Testament narrative? The Gospel of Matthew describes how at the moment of Jesus' death "the earth shook and the rocks split." Matthew also mentions a violent earthquake that took place at Jesus' tomb.

In Acts 4 we read of something that at least had the effect of an earthquake. After Peter and John made their dramatic appearance before the Sanhedrin and were released, the church held a prayer meeting. Acts 4:31 tells us that "the place where they were meeting was shaken."

These earthquakes apparently caused no loss of life or damage to property. They must have been localized tremors designed to remind men of God's awesome power. An earthquake of that kind could do us some good. If we have a careless, ho-hum attitude toward the Bible, the church, the Lord's Supper, and Jesus Christ himself, we may well pray, "Lord, send us such an earthquake!"

We need to be shaken into a fresh appreciation of Christ's death on the cross. We need to experience a brain-rattling awareness of the power of His resurrection. We would benefit

HYMN

"Revive Us Again"

Hallelujah! Thine the glory; Hallelujah! A-men! Hallelujah! Thine the glory; Revive us again.

~William P. Mackay

from a few spiritual shock waves awakening us to our responsibility to witness and serve.

Perhaps we prefer our observance of the Lord's Supper to be a calm, relaxed kind of experience. But we may have a greater need for a room-rocking reminder of the importance of personal holiness or a sanctuary-shaking summons to service.

PRAYER

Glorious Father in Heaven, we thank You for allowing us to dwell in relative safety. We would not pray for a literal earthquake with its terrible devastation. Give us instead a spiritual earthquake that will awaken us to our blessings and our duties. This Communion time would be ideal for such an awakening. In Jesus' name, amen.

Open Hymnal, Open Heart

PSALM 40:1-3

Do you have a favorite hymn that you enjoy singing at Communion time? Is it helpful in focusing your mind on the cross to sing George Bennard's familiar hymn, "The Old Rugged Cross"? Does your visit at the Lord's table give you a sense of being "Beneath the Cross of Jesus"? Can you say to Jesus as you hold the emblems, "Here, O My Lord, I See Thee Face to Face"? When Communion is over, are you moved to exclaim, "Oh, How He Loves You and Me"?

It can be beneficial as we commune to keep our hymnals open and handy. The hymn writers can give us the words we need to express our awe, our gratitude, and our love for the Lord. Leila Morris, for example, leads us in praying these words:

> Nearer, still nearer, nothing I bring,
> Naught as an off'ring to Jesus my King;
> Only my sinful, now contrite heart,
> Grant me the cleansing Thy blood doth impart.

What a prayer! What a beautiful expression of the spirit in which we must approach the Lord's Supper! What a magnifying of the name of Jesus! And many other hymns similarly lead

HYMN

"Nearer, Still Nearer"

*Nearer, still nearer,
close to Thy heart,
Draw me, my Savior,
so precious Thou art;
Fold me, O fold me
close to Thy breast,
Shelter me safe in that
"Haven of Rest,"
Shelter me safe in that
"Haven of Rest."*

~Leila N. Morris

us into the Communion service by calling us to quiet trust, humility, contrition, and gratitude.

Perhaps this morning would be a good time to lay an open hymnal on our lap as we commune. Our hands will be free to hold the emblems, while our eyes focus on those precious, poetic sentiments we have often sung. Let us join in their praises of the saving Christ and their prayers of simple confession.

PRAYER

We thank You, heavenly Father, for the great hymns that help us to express our faith. Help us to use them in demonstrating the kind of devotion to You and Your Son that is appropriate at this table. In Jesus' name, amen.

PASSOVER NIGHT —YOU ARE THERE!

1 CORINTHIANS 5:6, 7

The Lord's Supper was instituted at the close of Passover supper. First Corinthians 5:7 states that "Christ, our Passover lamb, has been sacrificed." It is appropriate, therefore, for us to draw some comparisons between Passover and the Lord's Supper.

Picture yourself inside an Israelite house on the first Passover night. The dozen or so people gathered here are safe from the terrible plague afflicting the Egyptians. The blood of the Passover lamb, smeared on the lintel and sideposts of the door, keeps them safe. We Christians enjoy safety from the plague of guilt and spiritual death, so long as we are protected by the blood of Jesus, the ultimate Lamb of God.

Within the Israelite home, the family members ate the flesh of the sacrificed lamb, along with unleavened bread and bitter herbs. We Christians partake of Christ, who is not only the Lamb of God, but also the true Bread of life. We are thereby strengthened for holy living and faithful service.

When the Israelites celebrated the original Passover, they were to be ready for travel. God had promised them release from their slavery, and a new homeland to inherit. The Passover

HYMN

"Hallelujah, What a Savior!"

When He comes, our glorious King, All His ransomed home to bring, Then anew this song we'll sing: Hallelujah! what a Savior!

~Philip P. Bliss

caused the Israelites to look ahead to Canaan, their future dwelling place.

When we participate in the Lord's Supper, we look ahead to Heaven, our ultimate home. In the heavenly scenes described in the book of Revelation, Jesus is frequently identified by His title, "the Lamb." We commune with the Lamb now around this earthly table. Someday, however, we will praise the Lamb in Heaven for being our sacrifice for sin.

PRAYER

Our heavenly Father, we give thanks to You for Jesus Christ, the Lamb of God. We praise You anew for His atoning blood. Stir up in us a keen anticipation for the day we praise the Lamb in Heaven. In Jesus' name, amen.

POUNDS OF BREAD, GALLONS OF JUICE

23

2 PETER 3:18

How much unleavened bread have you eaten at Communion services since you became a Christian? How much grape juice have you drunk? If as a longtime Christian you have been present regularly for Sunday Communion services, you may have eaten two or three pounds of unleavened bread and drunk two or three gallons of grape juice.

Of course there is not much benefit in working out such statistics. More important are the spiritual blessings you have gained through attendance at the Lord's table. Let us consider a few of these:

First, you have the simple benefit of a quiet time. Communion may give you your calmest, most peaceful moments of the week. If you work in a noisy factory, store, or office, that place is now far away. No radio or television set is blaring out loud music or distressing news, and no telephone is ringing.

Second, you enjoy fellowship with Jesus. This is the time of the week when you probably feel closest to your Savior. What a special joy it is to thank Him for His atoning death, to confess to Him last week's failures and struggles, and to promise Him a better effort at discipleship!

Third, you are able to share with Christian brothers and sisters. Here we come together

HYMN

"Bread of Heaven"

Bread of heav'n, on Thee we feed, For Thy flesh is meat indeed; Ever let our souls be fed With this true and living bread.

~Joseph Conder

with a common purpose: to partake of the same loaf and cup in remembrance of our crucified and risen Lord.

Pounds of bread, gallons of juice–the quantity does not matter. But the quality of past experiences at the Lord's table is significant. Let us thank God for the accumulated blessings in the hours spent at this table.

PRAYER

Gracious Father, we praise You for Communion services past and present. Help us to keep on adding to our treasure of moments at the table, communing with Your Son Jesus. In His name, amen.

24

RANKING THE ELEMENTS OF OUR WORSHIP

ACTS 2:42

Let us do some mental ranking of the elements of our worship. Most churches feature, in various arrangements, the following elements: call to worship, prayer, congregational singing, special music, Lord's Supper, offering, Scripture reading, sermon, invitation, benediction.

If we were to ask every member to list these elements in descending order of importance, we might obtain some unusual results. The ranking people might give the sermon could depend on whether or not the preacher told enough humorous stories. Some members would rate the congregational singing lower if their favorite hymns are not regularly sung. The benediction might appear close to the top. After all, quite a few folk are eager to head for the exits as soon as the last amen is said.

The Lord's Supper should appear as number one on every list. The New Testament indicates that this is the primary purpose for assembling on Sunday (Acts 20:7), and it should be the element in our service that touches us most deeply (1 Corinthians 10:16). We are communing with Jesus Christ at His table. The sermon, the singing, the prayers are all important, but they rank below this observance.

If anyone gives the Lord's Supper only a second or third place, what does it mean? It may

HYMN

"Communion Hymn"

On this Holy Lord's day morning, Master of the earth and sea; Stand we in Thy sacred presence, Hearts and souls athirst for Thee.

~Charles McMillan

mean that person is not adequately preparing his heart for communing with Jesus. The minister spends hours preparing his sermon, the musicians invest time in selecting and rehearsing the hymns. Each worshiper must also spend significant time readying his or her heart to partake of the emblems. When this is done, Communion is certain to be the high point of every worship service.

PRAYER

Our dear heavenly Father, we praise You, and we thank You for teaching us how to worship You. Guide us in approaching all of our worship, and especially the Lord's Supper, with careful preparation. In Jesus' name, amen.

Receiving, Followed by Giving

25

Acts 20:35

Jesus said it, and it must be true that "it is more blessed to give than to receive. " He certainly lived by this principle. There were, of course, the gifts of gold, frankincense, and myrrh He was given as an infant. People did contribute to His support during His ministry. Then, shortly before His death, He accepted the perfume Mary poured out on His body. But what He gave was so much, much more.

In many churches the worshipers are provided with a chance to receive before they give. That is, they receive the benefits afforded through observance of the Lord's Supper, and then they give their tithes and other financial gifts during the offering.

While such an order in public worship is not spelled out in Scripture, this is an appropriate way of arranging these elements. Jesus once exhorted His disciples, "Freely you have received, freely give" (Matthew 10:8). During Communion we remember the abundance of God's provision for us through Christ: forgiveness of sins, the indwelling of the Holy Spirit, the privilege of addressing God as Father, and the hope of eternal life.

Are we careful in our personal meditation during Communion to enumerate these blessings we have received? If so, we should be in

HYMN

"Something for Thee"

All that I am and have,—Thy gifts so free,—In joy, in grief, thro' life, Dear Lord, for Thee! And when Thy face I see, My ransomed soul shall be, Thro' all eternity, Something for Thee. Amen.

~Sylvanus D. Phelps

the proper frame of mind during the offering to give generously and sacrificially. One of our hymn writers has illustrated this connection very well in these words:

Savior, Thy dying love Thou gavest me,
Nor should I ought withhold, Dear Lord,
   from Thee:
In love my soul would bow,
My heart fulfill its vow,
Some off'ring bring Thee now,
Something for Thee.

PRAYER

Dear heavenly Father, our hearts are filled with joy as we ponder what You have given us. Inspire us to give as joyously as we have received. In Jesus' name, amen.

26

REPAIRING THE BELT

JOHN 13 :34, 35

A powerful motor, a gear mechanism, and a continuous belt—elder Maurice Strahle of Drexel Gardens Christian Church in Indianapolis, Indiana, referred to these to illustrate the importance of love in the church.

The motor, used in a coal-stripping operation in southern Indiana, seemed to have almost unlimited power. That represented the unlimited power God has, a power He makes available to His church.

The gear mechanism controlled the operations of the dragline machine: hoisting, dragging, swinging, lighting, and walking. These operations are reminders of the duties God has assigned His church: evangelism, teaching, worship, benevolent work, etc.

The continuous belt transferred the power from the motor to the gear mechanism. It symbolized the love that must exist in the church if God's power is to be used effectively in fulfilling the duties He has given us.

The belt was the source of many problems. A worker constantly had to adjust it to maintain the correct tension. Sometimes he had to treat it with resin or talcum powder to keep it from slipping. Occasionally the belt would tear and require mending. With all these problems, however, the worker never threw the belt away.

HYMN

"Blest Be the Tie That Binds"

Blest be the tie that binds Our hearts in Christian love; The fellowship of kindred minds Is like to that above.

~John Fawcett

In similar fashion we have problems in the church because we fail to love one another as we should. But God's power remains constant, and our responsibilities toward God do not change. We suffer from a "divine power slippage" when we neglect our brotherly and sisterly love. It is obvious that we need to be vigilant in "repairing the belt."

PRAYER

Our Father in Heaven, as we gather around the Lord's table, we commit ourselves to love. We focus our minds on Christ, of course. But help us also to think about our brothers and sisters in Christ and dedicate ourselves to loving them. In His name, amen.

27

RESOLVED TO REMEMBER

HEBREWS 10: 19-25

Does anyone take New Year's resolutions seriously? How often do we hear friends joking about how they made resolutions and then promptly broke them? They were going to lose some weight or give up an unhealthy habit like smoking or worrying. But after a few days or weeks that resolution was forgotten.

Here is a resolution we should all make. It does not involve any complicated procedures or strenuous work. What it does involve is the determination to say "No" to any temptation to break it. Here it is: "Resolved: I will, by the grace of God, be present each Sunday this year to commune with my Lord at His table."

Will you make that resolution? You may respond, "But what if we have unexpected company? How about those occasions in which we are up late on Saturday evening? Some weeks we are incredibly busy and want to do nothing but stay home on Sunday." The answer to these and other excuses is merely that the Lord's Supper should receive a high level of priority in our schedule.

Of course it is possible that illness or family emergencies or Sunday work required by our employer will cause us to break such a resolution. Nevertheless, it is a good idea to make it, trust God to help us keep it, and even if we

HYMN

"I Am Resolved"

I will hasten to Him, Hasten so glad and free; Jesus, Greatest, Highest, I will come to Thee.

~Palmer Hartsough

break it, commit ourselves to being present as often as possible.

PRAYER

Dear heavenly Father, we know we should plan to be present each Sunday so that we may partake of the Lord's Supper. But some are careless about attendance at this table. Help us right now to arrange our priorities and set up a schedule that will enable us to be here consistently. Then remind us of these priorities when we forget them. In Jesus' name, amen.

28

SEATED FOR SUPPER

MATTHEW 26:20

The seating arrangement at the original Lord's Supper was a matter of importance for the apostles. In his Studies in the Life of Christ, R. C. Foster suggests that all the apostles wanted to be as close to Jesus as possible. Some of them were probably a bit disgruntled by the seats they obtained, once the scrambling for places was completed.

What a contrast to the situation seen today! The Communion table, from which the bread and juice are distributed, is the nearest equivalent we have to Jesus' place at the original table. But in many churches worshipers sit as far away from the Communion table as they can.

Regardless of how the disciples were arranged at that original supper, one thing is clear: they sat (or rather, reclined) close to one another. They may not have cared for each others' company. After all, the band included rough fishermen, a traitorous tax collector, a fiery Zealot, and a betrayer-in-the-making. But to meet around one table, with Jesus at the head, meant reclining side by side.

Is our seating arrangement important? Does it matter how close to one another we sit as the emblems are passed to us? Is it right that any worshiper should be occupying a pew by himself

HYMN

"My Faith Looks Up to Thee"

My faith looks up to Thee, Thou Lamb of Calvary, Savior divine! Now hear me while I pray, Take all my guilt away, O let me from this day Be wholly Thine!

~Ray Palmer

or herself? Somehow it seems appropriate that we should be seated as close together as possible, demonstrating our unity in Jesus Christ, as we partake of these emblems.

PRAYER

Our gracious Father, we thank You for these intimate moments we may spend with Your Son at His table. Guide us in sharing with others the joy of our friendship with Jesus. In His name, amen.

29

SHARING OUR MEDITATIONS

PSALM 19:14

What goes on in the minds of worshipers
when the Communion service begins? If we
could somehow listen in on a congregation's
thoughts, would we hear something like the following? "I wish they would turn up the heat in
here!" "Look at that—there's a spot on my new
dress !" "I hope the preacher has a short sermon
today." "Hmm—where should we eat our
Sunday dinner?"

It may be inevitable that such thoughts will
cross our minds. However, it is likely that any
listener would also hear heart cries like these:
"Oh, Jesus, how can I thank You enough for
being my Savior?" "Lord, I come to You confess-
ing my embarrassment over the things I did last
week." "I need Your help badly right now, Jesus,
for I am facing powerful temptations."

What we think and feel during the Lord's
Supper is a private, personal, intimate occasion
of fellowship between us and our Savior. And
yet, sharing our meditations with fellow
Christians may be a way of edifying them.
Other believers may not understand how to
meditate. Offering them a glimpse of how we
commune with Jesus could help them.

This may serve as a reminder that we should
generally talk about our faith, our personal
Bible study and prayer, our struggles in resisting

HYMN

"Lord, Speak to Me"

*Lord, speak to me,
that I may speak In
living echoes of Thy
tone; As Thou hast
sought, so let me seek
Thy erring children
lost and lone.*

~Frances R. Havergal

temptations, our efforts at witnessing to friends and acquaintances. By discussing these and other aspects of our discipleship, we can strengthen and encourage fellow believers. Of course, it must not be a case of "Hey, look at me!" but of magnifying Jesus.

PRAYER

Our gracious Father, we thank You for these intimate moments we may spend with Your Son at His table. Guide us in sharing with others the joy of our friendship with Jesus. In His name, amen.

Silent Witnesses at Calvary

30

John 19:38-42

The Gospels do not tell us if Joseph of Arimathea and Nicodemus were present at the cross while Jesus was dying there. Probably they were not, since their relationship with Jesus was that of a secret, silent discipleship. However, soon after Jesus' death, they went into action. With Pilate's permission they took Jesus' body down from the cross, prepared it for burial, and placed it in Joseph's new tomb.

It is pointless to speculate over what the outcome of Jesus' trial before the Sanhedrin might have been, had these two men openly and actively supported Him. It was Jesus' destiny to go to the cross, and none of His disciples could have prevented that.

When we look at the kind of discipleship Joseph and Nicodemus practiced, we must say, "Am I like that? Have I been a secret, silent disciple? I know about how Jesus gave His life on the cross and arose from the tomb, but have I failed to share my witness with others?"

While Joseph and Nicodemus could not have prevented Jesus' death by openly professing Him, we can prevent something worse. Our silence can deprive friends and acquaintances of the gift of eternal life. But our decision to be bold, outspoken witnesses for Jesus Christ can

Hymn

"I Love to Tell the Story"

I love to tell the story, 'Twill be my theme in glory To tell the old, old story Of Jesus and His love.

~A. Catherine Hankey

prevent the tragedy of eternal loss for these persons.

Communion time is certainly an appropriate time to examine the quality of our witness. If we have been silent, let us be silent no more. If we have followed Jesus in a secret kind of way, let us resolve to bring our discipleship out into the open.

PRAYER

Our Father in Heaven, we thank You for the witness we bear every time we partake of these Communion emblems. But help us to also add the bold witness of our tongues and lips. In Jesus' name, amen.

31

Something
Better Than Fire

Matthew 28:1-7

Few events described in the Bible match the drama found in 1 Kings 18. Elijah painstakingly prepared his sacrifice on an altar on Mount Carmel. Then he offered a brief prayer to God as the assembled Israelites watched and listened. Then fire fell from Heaven, consuming the sacrifice, the altar, and the pools of water around the altar. Little wonder the Israelites were awed.

No fire will fall from Heaven today on our Communion table. We are not laying out a sacrifice; instead, we are remembering the greatest sacrifice of all. But we have no less drama here than in the hour of Elijah's offering on Mount Carmel.

It is certainly dramatic when a heroic individual marches courageously to face his moment of destiny. When Jesus entered Jerusalem on Palm Sunday, it seems that the shouts of the excited throngs must surely have been accompanied by the drum rolls of Heaven. Jesus was commencing a week that would conclude with His death and burial.

No other event in history holds the drama resurrection morning does. Imagine the guards outside Jesus' tomb as dawn approached. Perhaps they were struggling to stay awake. Possibly the morning was chill, and they were

Hymn

"Christ Arose!"

Up from the grave He arose, With a mighty triumph o'er His foes; He arose a Victor from the dark domain, And He lives forever with His saints to reign. He arose! He arose! Hallelujah! Christ arose!

~Robert Lowry

flexing their arms and legs to warm their flesh. Then it happened! A shining angel appeared! He rolled the stone from the tomb's entrance, revealing an empty grave!

Let us therefore feel the drama surrounding this observance of the Lord's Supper. Let us approach the table, tingling with the thrill of it. And let us resolve to share the excitement of Calvary and the empty tomb with our neighbors.

PRAYER

Our Father in Heaven, we express our gratitude for the powerful combination of the cross and the empty tomb. Stir us continually to excitement over these dramatic events portrayed in our Communion. In Jesus' name, amen.

32

SPENDING CHRISTMAS AT CALVARY

GALATIANS 4:4, 5

Every year Christmas seems to become more of a heathen holiday, further removed from the celebration of Christ's birth. Of course, the New Testament does not exhort us to remember Christ's birth, but rather His death. And yet, Christmas, with the world still focusing to some extent on the birth of a special Child two thousand years ago, offers great potential for spiritual blessing.

We must not allow ourselves to separate Christ from Calvary. If the baby in the manger was only an ordinary baby, cute and cuddly, He has no more significance to us than billions of other babies born since His time. But since He was born to die an atoning death for our sins on Calvary, His birth and infancy, His boyhood and adulthood, all take on a tremendous significance.

Let us spend this Christmas at Calvary. As we receive the emblems of His supper, it is appropriate to recall the scenes of Jesus' birth and infancy. But it is vital that we connect them with the tumultuous events that took place some thirty years later.

And so let us remember how the Christ-child, lovingly wrapped in swaddling clothes, would one day have His clothing stripped from Him and His back exposed to the cruel lash. Let us

HYMN

"Silent Night! Holy Night!"

Silent night, holy night, All is calm, all is bright Round yon virgin mother and child. Holy infant so tender and mild, Sleep in heavenly peace, Sleep in heavenly peace.

~Joseph Mohr

recall how He who was surrounded by the protecting wood of a manger would someday be stretched against the rough wood of a cross. Let us ponder again how the One who was adored by shepherds and wise men would at last be subjected to ridicule by the hateful throngs at Calvary.

Prayer

Our Father, we praise You for the exciting story of Jesus' birth. Help us to remind ourselves and others that a Savior was born in Bethlehem. May that reminder be vivid in our minds as we partake of these emblems. In Jesus' name, amen.

33

THE AWESOME CROSS

MARK 15:37-39

The centurion who cried out at the moment of Jesus' death was obviously in awe of what he had seen. Jesus' noble deportment on the cross, the manner in which He yielded up His spirit, and the earthquake that occurred when Jesus died drew forth from the Roman officer those remarkable words, "Surely this man was the Son of God!"

Are we in awe of the cross? Probably not, since it is such an over-exposed symbol today. Where have you seen crosses lately? On church buildings and religious signs, of course. Along the roadsides, marking the sites of fatal automobile accidents. On necklaces worn often by people who make no pretense of being Christians. How can we be in awe of the cross when it is used in such a variety of ways?

The symbol of the cross must remind us of the One who hung on a cross two thousand years ago. Think of it—the Son of God was crucified! The centurion probably did not comprehend what he was saying. Indeed, some modern translations of the New Testament have him exclaiming, "This was a son of God." But we know that it was the unique, only-begotten Son of God who died on that cross, and that is awesome!

HYMN

"In the Cross of Christ"

In the cross of Christ I glory, Tow'ring o'er the wrecks of time; All the light of sacred story Gathers round its head sublime.

~John Bowring

We should likewise be in awe of these Communion reminders of the cross. It is merely bread and grape juice of which we are about to partake. However, it points us back to a body slain and blood shed on that awesome cross. Let us therefore partake in a sense of wonder and amazement.

PRAYER

Our Father, how awesome is Your plan of salvation! We thank You for the cross, and even more for the One who hung on Calvary's cross. Stir us to continual wonder at the thought of Calvary. In Jesus' name, amen.

The Bank Employee's Meditation

2 Timothy 1:12

It is often said that we practice faith in some form every day of our lives. One example of this is in our dealing with our local bank. We deposit money into a savings account, or we invest in a certificate of deposit. Then we trust that our bank will not only keep the money safe that we have deposited, but will also earn us a significant amount of interest.

Those who work in banks try to convey to their customers a sense of trustworthiness and dependability. Imagine going to your bank and seeing the manager dressed up like a riverboat gambler, or watching the clerk take your deposit money and stuff it into her purse. You would be likely to find a new bank very quickly.

We have made a far more important deposit. In becoming Christians we have entrusted to Jesus Christ our hopes for eternal life. He has proved himself trustworthy and dependable. Anyone who is willing to lay down his life on our behalf, as Jesus did, is surely someone we can trust.

Perhaps we can look upon the Lord's Supper as a kind of statement of our account.

Each week we are given a fresh reminder of our faith-deposit in Christ. The emblems we partake of picture His beaten body and shed blood, and in turn they remind us of how far

Hymn

"I Know Whom I Have Believed"

But "I know whom I have believed, and am persuaded that He is able To keep that which I've committed Unto Him against that day."

~Daniel W. Whittle

He has gone to earn our trust. Each week we meet with the living Christ at His table and are made freshly aware of the eternal life in Heaven He is holding in store for us.

PRAYER

Our gracious Father in Heaven, thank You for giving us good reason to trust in You and in Your Son Jesus. Help us to strengthen our trust and confidence as we partake of these emblems. We pray in Jesus' name. Amen.

35

THE BEST COMMUNION SERVICE EVER

MATTHEW 26:29

What is the best, the most memorable, the most inspiring Communion service in which you have taken part?

Some Christians might answer this question in terms of size. Approximately forty thousand worshipers shared the Lord's Supper in the opening service of the 1995 North American Christian Convention in Indianapolis. It would be legitimate to list this as the best because it is an awesome experience to be among such a mighty gathering of partakers.

Other Christians might respond that a small, intimate gathering of believers provided the right atmosphere for their best Communion service ever. Perhaps it was a family circle, made necessary by severe weather that prevented attendance at church. It may have been a Sunday school class on a weekend camping excursion, partaking of the emblems with the music of nature in the background.

Some may best recall their first occasion of Communion, either on the day of their confession of faith and baptism into Christ or on the Sunday following those momentous events. Having so recently tasted the sweet joy of forgiveness and cleansing through Jesus' shed blood, they saw a particular significance in partaking for the first time of the loaf and cup.

HYMN

"When We All Get to Heaven"

When we all get to heaven, What a day of rejoicing that will be! When we all see Jesus, We'll sing and shout the victory.

~Eliza E. Hewitt

The truth is that the best Communion service ever is the one described in the Scripture read earlier. When we drink the fruit of the vine with Jesus Christ in His Father's completed kingdom, it will be the most emotionally-moving reminder ever of the redeeming power of His death on the cross.

Let us partake this morning in keen anticipation of that Communion service to come.

PRAYER

Our gracious heavenly Father, thank You for the promise of the Communion service above. We know that our observance of the Lord's Supper today is also very special. Help us to approach it as a tremendous privilege. In Jesus' name, amen.

36

THE FACTORY WORKER'S MEDITATION

ACTS 20:7

Assemble, solder, grind, polish—these are some of the tasks of the factory worker. Over and over, day after day, week after week, he or she repeats the same productive actions. Modern factories at least provide a safe and relatively comfortable setting for such work, and workers often receive generous break times away from the routine. But the repetition does grow wearisome at times.

What we are about to do is a matter of repetition. If you have been faithful in your attendance at the Lord's table, you are in the habit of eating a small piece of Communion bread and drinking from the cup of grape juice. But surely this repetition is never a wearisome or tedious activity.

Every Communion service is similar in a way, but every one is also different. Today you probably come to the Lord's table in a somewhat different mood than you did a week ago. Perhaps the week between has featured some unique blessings, and you come to the table with a heart overflowing with thanksgiving and praise. Or perhaps the past week has left you with heavy burdens, and in communing with your Lord you seek His comfort and encouragement.

Whatever you may be feeling at the moment, do not let this Communion be a mere repetition

HYMN

"Safely Through Another Week"

Safely through another week God has brought us on our way; Let us now a blessing seek, Waiting in His courts today; Day of all the week the best, Emblem of eternal rest: Day of all the week the best, Emblem of Eternal rest.

~John Newton

of actions you have taken dozens or scores or hundreds of times before. Confess last week's sins, lay last week's burdens upon the Lord, thank Him for last week's victories, commit to Him this week's plans.

PRAYER

Our loving Father in Heaven, we come to this table as we have on many previous occasions. But this meeting around the Lord's table is once again unique and special. Help us to be alert and thoughtful as we partake. We ask it in the name of our divine host Jesus. Amen.

37

THE FATHER'S MEDITATION

MATTHEW 3:13-17

The Gospels describe two dramatic occasions when the Father spoke from Heaven regarding Jesus with the words, "This is my beloved Son, in whom I am well pleased." The first was following Jesus' baptism; the second was during His transfiguration.

It is not recorded that the Father spoke these words while Jesus was being crucified.

In one way the words might have seemed inappropriate. Jesus while on the cross became the embodiment of sin, according to 2 Corinthians 5:21. He also became the focus of the curse that sin brought with it, according to Galatians 3:13. Nevertheless, the Father was pleased with His Son at Calvary, because Jesus was rendering perfect obedience in submitting to the cross.

The heavenly Father is pleased by obedience. Earthly fathers understand that, because they also take pleasure in their children's obedience. To obey is to exhibit trust, respect, submission, and commitment. When children fail to obey, they must receive punishment. Neither the heavenly Father nor earthly fathers delight in administering punishment.

We will not hear a voice from Heaven today, praising us for our obedience in meeting around this table. But we can be sure that our

HYMN

"Trust and Obey"

Trust and obey, for there's no other way To be happy in Jesus, But to trust and obey. Amen.

~John H. Sammis

Father is pleased that we have made this Communion service a priority. His Son has commanded us, "Do this in remembrance of me," and we are obeying that command.

The Father and the Son will be further pleased if we use this time of partaking to pledge ourselves to childlike obedience in all phases of our lives. Let us do so, as we engage in our own personal meditation.

PRAYER

Our Father, You are the perfect example of fatherhood. You are worthy of our prompt obedience. May we learn to give You the kind of obedience Jesus gave, the obedience illustrated by these Communion emblems. In His precious name, amen.

THE IMPORTANCE OF EAGER DESIRE

38

LUKE 22:14, 15

Why was Jesus so eager to share the Passover supper with His apostles? Did He need this consoling companionship before He faced alone His trials and the cross? Was this an occasion on which He expected to impart many valuable lessons to them? Did He view this as a vital time of fortifying them for the profound grief they were soon to experience?

Whatever the reason, Jesus came to the Passover table with an eager desire to participate in its benefits. Do we come to the Lord's table with a similar eager desire? Are we excited and enthusiastic about sharing in this service?

Every one of us must admit to an eager desire for something. It may be directed toward a material item: a home, an automobile, a recreational vehicle, or a computer system. It may be focused on some pleasurable experience: our Sunday dinner, watching a ball game, visiting with family members or old friends, or reading a good book.

The eagerness with which we come to the Lord's table should be more intense than our feelings for any of these. We should so desire to be here that we will let no trivial matter keep us from communing with our Lord. It is vital that we have an earnest longing for this supper,

HYMN

"O to Be Like Thee!"

O to be like Thee! blessed Redeemer, This is my constant longing and prayer; Gladly I'll forfeit all of earth's treasures, Jesus, Thy perfect likeness to wear.

~Thomas O. Chisholm

so that when we commune, we will allow nothing to distract us from our worship.

Let us take inventory of our priorities, and let us aim to develop an eager desire for communing and worship.

PRAYER

Our dear Father in Heaven, how thankful we are for Jesus' desire to do Your will, and for His eagerness to share life's experiences with people like us. Guide us in directing our desire, so that it may focus on communing with Him and serving Him faithfully. We pray in His name. Amen.

THE MAILMAN'S MEDITATION

39

ACTS 10:34-36, 43

A mail carrier often receives undeserved credit or blame. Imagine such a messenger, with a hopeful expression, handing a sheaf of mail to a man and being angrily informed, "You didn't bring me the check I'm expecting!" Or picture him giving a letter to an elderly lady and hearing her exclaim, "A letter from my grandsons. Oh, thank you, Mr. Jones!" Surely any longtime mail carrier has had many such experiences.

There is good news and bad news to deliver. We tend to think of Jesus as a bringer of good news. We are aware that the word "gospel" means "good news." But Jesus has also brought bad news. He had a great deal to say about God's judgment against sin and sinners. He spoke about Hell. He called human beings to repentance and reformation of life.

At Communion time we want to meditate on good news: Jesus' victory over sin and death, our salvation, our hope of eternal life in Heaven. But we may need to think about some bad news also. If we have been careless about indulging in sin, the bad news is that God still hates sin and is angry with it. He still judges sin and the sinner.

With the gospel the good news prevails. We can deal with the bad news of sin, judgment, and Hell by trusting and obeying God,

HYMN

"Wonderful Words of Life"

Beautiful words, wonderful words, Wonderful words of Life.

~Philip P. Bliss

83

repenting of our lapses into sin, and recommitting ourselves to Christian living. Then the good news of salvation and eternal life will ring out again in our hearts and minds.

PRAYER

Dear heavenly Father, we praise You anew for the good news of Jesus' atoning death and triumphant resurrection. Guide us in cherishing this good news and in shaping our lives around it. We offer our prayer in Jesus' name. Amen.

40

THE MOTHER'S MEDITATION

JOHN 19:25-27

It has to be a bitter experience for a mother to lose a son or daughter: to see all her efforts at nurturing, guiding, encouraging, and disciplining swept away in a moment's time; to have the object of her loving concern torn from her; to know that she will never again on earth witness that special smile or hear that familiar voice or feel that tender embrace.

Perhaps only a mother who has suffered such a loss can understand what Mary felt.

For some thirty years she felt pride, concern, gratitude, bewilderment, and dozens of other emotions as she saw her son grow from infancy to childhood to young manhood to full maturity. And then the worst possible event, the unthinkable, occurred: her son was nailed to a cross.

Jesus cared about His mother. Even as He was dying, He tried to cushion the pain of her bereavement by entrusting her to His beloved disciple John. Jesus likewise cares about all mothers, fathers, and children who suffer. He had earlier felt the pain of death's separation. His earthly father Joseph apparently died during Jesus' teenage years or shortly afterward. His cousin John the Baptist was murdered by Herod Antipas. His good friend Lazarus died, and John's Gospel tells us that upon reaching the tomb of Lazarus, "Jesus wept."

We commune at the Lord's Supper with a Savior who cares. We can bring our pains, our griefs, our frustrations, and our anger at what life has dealt out to us, and He will give sweet relief.

Prayer

Our Father in Heaven, we thank You for giving us comfort, assurance, and strength. Most of us here have at some time experienced severe suffering. It is a joy to know we have a Father and a Savior who care. In Jesus' name, amen.

41

THE MYSTERY OF THE MISSING FIVE THOUSAND

MARK 6:39-44; 15:12-15

In all four Gospels we read the account of Jesus' miraculous feeding of the five thousand. And in all four Gospels we read of another crowd that thronged Pilate's place of judgment. This crowd cried out for Barabbas, rather than Jesus, to be released. Here is a mystery: what happened to the five thousand who had witnessed Jesus' power? Why were they not present to give Him support at the time of His condemnation?

The sixth chapter of John gives us at least a partial answer to this mystery. Some of those who were miraculously fed wanted to make Jesus an earthly king. But He resisted that effort and described His mission as spiritual rather material or political. As a result these people turned away from Him.

At this moment we must be more concerned with the missing dozens or scores who should be assembled with us around the Lord's table. We must ask, "Why are those who identify themselves as Christ's followers not present to commune with Him?" Are people still permitting material and physical interests to take priority over the spiritual? Obviously, they are.

Of course we can commune with our Lord, whether we be in an assembly of one thousand, one hundred, or twenty. But it should nevertheless trouble us that fellow believers are not here with us to honor and obey the Lord. It is well that we commit ourselves to contacting these missing ones. Let us implore them, "Come to Jesus' table, join us in communing with Him, show Him the faithfulness He deserves."

PRAYER

Our heavenly Father, thank You for Jesus' faithfulness in fulfilling His mission, even when human beings proved unfaithful to Him. Impress us with the importance of our being faithful in this practice of weekly communing at His table. In His name, amen.

THE SCHOOLTEACHER'S MEDITATION

42

JOHN 7:14-17

Jesus is our teacher, and surely He means to teach us at His table. We do not set up a chalkboard for Him to use or a projector and screen or an easel and notepad. He has all the teaching tools He needs in the Communion emblems.

He teaches us by means of the bread. In the Bible, bread occupies a major role. On the night of the first Passover the enslaved Israelites ate unleavened bread. When the prophet Elijah was hiding from the evil King Ahab and Queen Jezebel, God sent ravens to him with bread. The bread of the presence was on display in the temple.

All of this has a connection with Jesus Christ. He is the true bread, the spiritual bread that nourishes and sustains men's hungry souls. In a moment we will hold a piece of the Communion bread. Let us focus on it and allow Jesus to teach us something of its vast significance.

He teaches us by means of the juice. We know that blood is a prominent topic in the Bible. The small amount of grape juice we will soon hold can remind us of the many blood sacrifices offered under the Old Testament. Jesus wants to teach us how His own blood supersedes the blood of bulls and goats and other sacrificial animals.

HYMN

"More About Jesus"

More, more about Jesus, More, more about Jesus; More of His saving fullness see, More of His love who died for me.

~Eliza E. Hewitt

We do not bring an apple to place on our teacher's table. We must bring something better: our hearts and our minds and our wills, ready to be instructed and molded by the Master Teacher.

PRAYER

We have come to this table, heavenly Father, to commune with Your Son and to be taught. May our hearts be open to the riches of Jesus' instruction. We pray in His precious name. Amen.

THE SECRETARY'S MEDITATION

43

COLOSSIANS 3:23, 24

"Miss Smith, would you please call our accountant and set up an appointment for me?" "Mrs. Jones, I want you to send a copy of our product catalog to those prospective customers." "Ms. Johnson, please call up the Williams' account on the computer."

These requests are typical ones given to the present-day secretary. Many men serve as secretaries. However, when we hear the word "secretary," we usually think of a woman with a friendly smile, a cheery voice, and an efficient manner, performing the bidding of her boss or bosses.

It is not an exaggeration to say that we all are Jesus' secretaries. The term is related to the word "secret." A secretary handles someone's secret or private business. Unfortunately, the fact that Jesus Christ died for our sins and rose again is a secret too many people do not know. We need to handle Jesus' "secret" business and make it public, to inform increasing numbers of human beings of His gift of salvation.

And we need to be His secretaries by doing His bidding generally. He wants us to remind one another that we have an appointment with Him at His table. He desires that we participate in the business of communicating His word. He is concerned that we pray for one another and

HYMN

"It Pays to Serve Jesus"

It pays to serve Jesus, it pays ev'ry day, It pays ev'ry step of the way; Tho' the pathway to glory may sometimes be drear, You'll be happy each step of the way.

~Frank C. Huston

help one another keep our spiritual accounts in order.

As we commune today, it is well for us to say to our Lord, "What duties do You have for me to perform? What assignments do You want me to undertake? Help me to be Your faithful secretary."

PRAYER

Our dear heavenly Father, thank You for the privilege of doing Jesus' business. His business is saving the lost, and we are grateful that we have obtained that salvation. Guide us as we do the bidding of our Savior. In His name, amen.

44

THE SPIRITUAL SIDE OF SELF

MATTHEW 16:24-28

Think for a moment of all those hyphenated words that begin with "self." On the positive side we might list self-sacrifice, self-denial, and self-control. Clearly negative would be self-pity, self-satisfaction, and self-exaltation.

Communion time calls us to deal with the sinful views of self. Jesus said we must take up our cross, which speaks of self-denial and self-sacrifice, and leaves no room for self-satisfaction. If we are inclined to excessive pride in ourselves because of our education or our income or our physical appearance or anything else, now is the time to forsake that. Let us humble ourselves before our heavenly Father and our Savior Jesus Christ.

Perhaps self-pity is our problem. We moan inwardly over how unfairly life has treated us. We wallow in our woes over family problems, financial crises, difficulties in the church, and the like. Self-pity accomplishes nothing. Let us relinquish it and renew our trust in our loving Father's care.

We may have a habit of self-exaltation. Many of our problems arise because we always have to be first, best, or the center of attention. We want glory, adulation, praise from others. Let us make this the moment when we give the glory

HYMN

"Jesus, I My Cross Have Taken"

Jesus, I my cross have taken, All to leave, and follow Thee; Destitute, despised, forsaken, Thou, from hence, my all shalt be: Perish ev'ry fond ambition, All I've sought, and hoped, and known; Yet how rich is my condition, God and heav'n are still my own!

~Henry F. Lyte

to God. Let us exalt His name and commit ourselves to doing what will please Him.

The Communion emblems call us to a healthy self-denial and self-sacrifice. Let us heed their call.

PRAYER

We praise You again, heavenly Father, for an old rugged cross and an empty tomb. Help us to remember that while Jesus bore the agony of the cross in a never-to-be-repeated act of sacrifice, we also have a cross to bear. Guide us, as we partake of these emblems, to commit ourselves to the sacrifices we must make. In the name of Jesus our Savior, amen.

The Store Clerk's Meditation

MARK 10:45

If we do much shopping, we may be inclined to say that good service is extremely rare anymore. Perhaps we have had the experience of dealing with store clerks who were rude and seemingly disinterested in selling us anything.

Surely those Christians who work as store clerks are not like that. They greet customers with a warm smile and the cheerful words, "Good morning. How may I serve you?" And they do this not merely in the interest of good salesmanship, but because they are committed to service.

Jesus Christ greets us every Sunday by saying in effect, "Good morning! How may I serve you?" When we meet Him at His table, we acknowledge one major way in which He has already served us. He gave His life as a ransom for us, and the loaf and the cup are reminders of the ransom price.

But Jesus Christ continues to serve us. He is with us, whenever two or three of us come together in His name, as Matthew 18:20 tells us. He is living in each one of us, according to Galatians 2:20. Hebrews 7:25 informs us that He makes intercession on our behalf. In Philippians 4:13 we are assured that He strengthens us.

HYMN

"O Master, Let Me Walk With Thee"

O Master, let me walk with Thee In lowly paths of service free; Tell me Thy secret; help me bear The strain of toil, the fret of care.

~Washington Gladden

At Communion time we are served. Those who prepare the emblems, those who pray over them, and those who distribute them serve us. More importantly, Jesus Christ serves us. Let us accept all this service gratefully, and then let us dedicate ourselves to serving as we have been served.

PRAYER

Our gracious Father, we thank You for the many ways we have been served. We especially praise You for the service Jesus Christ has given and continues to give us. May these moments of Communion stir us to Christ-like service on behalf of others. In Jesus' name, amen.

THE SYMBOLISM OF SNOW

46

PSALM 51:7; ISAIAH 1:18

For a significant part of the United States of America, wintertime features lengthy periods when snow lies deep on the ground. Many citizens of the "snowbelt" complain that the white stuff is a nuisance. It makes driving difficult. It must be removed from driveways and sidewalks. It can sting the face and obscure the vision of a person walking through a fierce snowstorm.

But most people will admit that snow has one notable benefit: it covers the bleakness and ugliness of the barren earth with a smooth, glistening coat. When fresh on the earth, it radiates an appearance of crystalline purity. And that is not to be forgotten, even when it later turns to an unsightly, gray slush.

We Christians can view newly-fallen snow and exclaim, "My soul is as pure and white as this fresh snow! I have been cleansed of sin through the shed blood of Jesus Christ!" Even if we live in an area where snow is rare, it is easy for us to close our eyes and picture ourselves looking out a window at pure, white snow. Then we can appreciate David's prayer to be washed whiter than snow, and God's promise through Isaiah to make scarlet sins as white as snow.

HYMN

"Whiter Than Snow"

Whiter than snow, yes, whiter than snow; Now wash me, and I shall be whiter than snow.

~James Nicholson

The loaf, the cup, and snow—what a combination! Let us partake in a fresh sense of recognition that we have been purified, cleansed, and renewed through the atoning blood of Jesus Christ.

PRAYER

Our heavenly Father, we thank You for the illustrations of spiritual truths You provide in nature. We thank You specifically for snow, whether it lies on the ground outside our place of meeting or must simply be pictured in our minds. May it vividly demonstrate to us what You have done for our souls through Jesus Christ. In His name, amen.

TISSUES FOR TEARS?

47

REVELATION 21:1-4

Elder Harold Griffey of Drexel Gardens Christian Church in Indianapolis, Indiana, began his Communion meditation: "If there is a stock market in Heaven, the Kimberly-Clark Corporation's stock will be the best buy. They make tissue products, and there will surely be a lot of those needed. After all, the Bible says that God will wipe every tear from our eyes."

What kinds of tears will God wipe away? Revelation 21:4 refers to sorrow and pain, which cause many tears. These will no longer exist. Our new bodies will not be subject to pain. Our heavenly Father will supply every need, so we will never cry over the loss of material things. And there will be no death and no more occasion to mourn the death of a loved one.

How about tears of relief? It seems possible that we will shed these when we finally complete the trials and sufferings of earthly life.

How about tears of joy? Our reunion in Heaven with family and friends and our long-awaited experience of seeing our Savior would seem likely to move us to tears.

Whether or not tissues will be used, God will have plenty of tears to wipe away. In the meantime we occasionally weep. Perhaps we are moved to tears at Communion time. We may

HYMN

"Come, Ye Disconsolate"

Come, ye disconsolate, where'er ye languish; Come to the mercy seat, fervently kneel; Here bring your wounded hearts, Here tell your anguish; Earth has no sorrow that Heav'n cannot heal.

~Thomas Moore

weep in sorrow when we think of the suffering our sins caused our Savior or when we remember anew how our guilt has been taken away through Jesus' shed blood. And we may have tears of joy in contemplating how we shall behold Him in Heaven.

PRAYER

Our Father in Heaven, thank You for tears of relief and joy, and for comforting us when we have shed tears of sorrow and grief. As we partake of these emblems, help us to set our hearts on that place where You will wipe all bitter tears away. In Jesus' name, amen.

48

TRAGIC TABLE MANNERS

1 CORINTHIANS 11:23-29

"Don't chew with your mouth open." "Say 'Please' and 'Thank you' and 'Excuse me.'" "Take all you want, but eat all you take." From childhood we have had such rules impressed on us. Our parents wanted us to practice good table manners.

Since Communion time is a matter of approaching the Lord's table, it is obvious that table manners are also important here. Some members of the church in Corinth were guilty of tragic table manners. We do not want that to be true of us.

What kind of table manners do we need to keep in mind? The simple matter of considerateness toward our Host is one. If we are invited to a banquet or formal dinner, we will try to arrange our schedule so that we may attend. Are we rude to our Host Jesus Christ in thoughtlessly failing to attend this supper to which He invites us?

Another violation of table manners is taking the Lord's Supper lightly. The Corinthians were overlooking the rich symbolism of Christ's slain body and shed blood. We are equally in danger of popping the bread in our mouth and gulping down the grape juice without seriously thinking about Jesus Christ's suffering on our behalf.

HYMN

"Jesus, the Very Thought of Thee"

Jesus, the very thought of Thee With sweetness fills my breast; But sweeter far Thy face to see, And in Thy presence rest.

~Edward Caswall

At this table as at the dinner table we should speak graciously. We should say, "Thank You, Jesus. Please help me to be a better Christian. Excuse me when I fail to conduct myself as I should."

PRAYER

Gracious Father in Heaven, we praise You for the privilege of assembling around Your Son's table. We are aware that we must come here reverently, attentively, and expectantly. Help us to do so, and may we thereby show our Host how deeply we appreciate His invitation. We pray in Jesus' name. Amen.

49

WAITING AT THE TABLE

PSALM 130:5

Few things we do can be more tedious than waiting. We visit a restaurant and wait to be served. We go to the bank and wait in line. We keep a doctor's appointment and still have to wait, because an emergency has put the doctor behind schedule.

In various places the Bible writers instruct us to wait on God. That may be a type of instruction that we tend to resist. Something inside us cries out, "Why must we wait on God to answer our prayers, rescue us from painful trials, and grant us long-sought blessings?" But whether we like it or not, we must wait.

When the emblems of the Lord's Supper are distributed, we must wait again. Perhaps we are eager to take hold of these special emblems and use them in communing with our Savior. Perhaps, on the other hand, we sit in a comparatively remote part of the church auditorium just so we will have more time to meditate before the emblems reach us.

Whatever the cause for our waiting at the Lord's table, it offers us a tremendous opportunity to cultivate our habit of waiting on the Lord. Here we can pray, "O Lord, I acknowledge that You know best. I affirm again my trust in You and my hope in Your word. I wait on You,

HYMN

"Near the Cross"

Jesus, keep me near the cross, There a precious fountain Free to all, a healing stream, Flows from Calv'ry's mountain.

~Fanny J. Crosby

assured that You will meet my needs in Your own way and in your own time."

PRAYER

Our heavenly Father, we thank You for the many times before when we have waited on You and received a blessing. We confess that in spite of that we still tend to be fretful and impatient. As we wait at this table, remind us again of Your wisdom, Your goodness, and Your love for us. We offer our prayer in Jesus' name. Amen.

WHAT WILL YOU SAY TO JESUS?

50

JOHN 20:24-29

We are going to have a "Thomas experience. "Like the apostle Thomas, we have often heard from others about the risen Christ. And like him we are one day going to behold Jesus Christ with our own eyes. We shall see for ourselves the evidence of the nails in His hands and feet and the spear wound in His side. Surely we will be led, as Thomas was, to exclaim, "My Lord and my God!"

What else will we say to Jesus on that day? It is profitable to ponder that question. We may find it worthwhile to rehearse what we will say. On the other hand, we may want to wait for that glorious moment and let an overflowing heart direct the movement of our lips.

If you were in Jesus' presence right now, what would you say? It might be something like this: "Lord, I am unworthy of what You have done for me by dying for my sins. But I thank You, Lord, for Your precious gift of salvation. Now I just want to love You and praise You and serve You forever and forever."

Of course you are in Jesus' presence right now. This is His table. He is the Host, and you are one of His guests. You can commune personally with Him in these moments of meditation before and after you partake of the loaf

HYMN

"Here, O My Lord, I See Thee Face to Face"

Here, O my Lord, I see Thee face to face; Here would I touch and handle things unseen; Here grasp with firmer hand th' eternal grace, And all my weariness upon Thee lean.

~Horatius Bonar

and the cup. Say to Him now what you will someday tell Him face-to-face in Heaven.

PRAYER

Our Father in Heaven, we thank You for the glorious prospect of beholding You and Your Son in Heaven. Here at this table we enjoy a sweet foretaste of that eternal access to Your presence. Help us in these moments to commune with Your Son and to communicate our love and gratitude to Him. In His name, amen.

WHERE WERE YOU?

51

JOHN 14:15

Many people who were living in 1941 can tell you just where they were when they first learned of the Japanese attack on Pearl Harbor. Those who were alive in 1963 probably recall what they were doing when word came of the assassination of President John F. Kennedy. And people remember the circumstances in which they heard of the more recent tragedy, the explosion of the Challenger spacecraft in 1986.

If someone were to ask, "Where were you on such-and-such a Sunday morning?" we should be able to give a very specific answer: "I was present for the worship service at church, and I partook of the emblems of the Lord's Supper." Of course, we may not always be able to say precisely which church we attended. But if we have been conscientious about meeting the Lord at His table, it does not matter whether that table was in our hometown or elsewhere.

We often say that the Lord's Supper is the focal point of our worship service. What we are saying now is that it should be the focal point of our life. When we can say where we were and what we were doing during the first morning of every week of our adult lives, that is something significant.

One of the best things that can happen during this Communion service is for each of us to

HYMN

"O Jesus, I Have Promised"

O Jesus, I have promised To serve Thee to the end; Be Thou forever near me, My Master and my Friend: I shall not fear the battle If Thou art by my side, Nor wander from the pathway If Thou wilt be my guide.

~John E. Bode

promise the Lord to be present as often as possible at His table. Then if someone asks us, "Where were you?" we can promptly answer, "I was communing with my Lord at His table."

PRAYER

We are present at this table today, heavenly Father, and we know this is where we should be each Sunday. Thank You for the privilege of partaking. Remind us regularly of the responsibility of partaking. In Jesus' name, amen.

52

WILL HE COME AT COMMUNION TIME?

MATTHEW 24:42-44

Adolphus Perkins was an elder years ago at the Christian Church in Lawrence, Indiana. He frequently expressed his conviction that when Jesus comes again, it will be at Communion time. That is an interesting idea to ponder.

Some questions come to mind: Will He come according to Eastern Standard Time, Central Standard Time, or some other? Will His timetable fit those churches that have Communion before the sermon or after it? And how about those churches that have more than one worship service?

All of this is not to ridicule that elder's idea, but merely to note some problems associated with it. But it also brings to mind several positive aspects: We could go directly from this simple supper to the marriage feast of the Lamb. We could be transported from handling the emblematic bread into the presence of Him who is the Living Bread. We could make the transition from drinking the emblematic grape juice to witnessing Him whose blood has cleansed us from sin.

This much is certain: There is no more appropriate time than Communion time to focus on the fact of Jesus' promised return. The hymn title asks, "Will Jesus find us watching?" If we are meeting regularly at the Lord's table,

HYMN

"Will Jesus Find Us Watching?"

Oh, can we say we are ready, brother? Ready for the soul's bright home? Say, will He find you and me still watching, Waiting, waiting when the Lord shall come?

~Fanny J. Crosby

we will be more likely to be alert for His return.
Whether He comes on a Sunday during the
worship service or in the middle of the week,
we who have been faithful in communing with
Him are watching and waiting through that act.

PRAYER

Our Father in Heaven, we praise You for the
precious promise of Jesus' return. And we are
thankful for the way the Lord's Supper reminds
us of that event and helps us to prepare for it.
As we take the bread and the juice, help us to
be watchful. In Jesus' name, amen.

INDEX OF SCRIPTURES

(Note: The number after each Scripture reference is the number of the meditation in which the Scripture is used.)

INDEX OF HYMNS

(Note: The number after each hymn is the number of the meditation in which the hymn is used.)